Maximize
Motherhood
A 30-Day Devotional

Practical Encouragement for Each Day

Deb Ober

For Holly, Brittany, Justin and Brooke.

Being your mom is the sweetest gift of my life.
From late-night feedings to kitchen dancing and algebra lessons, I wouldn't trade a moment of this beautiful journey with you.

Thank you for the privilege of being your mom, and for teaching me something new each day.
I look forward joyfully to all the new memories we will make together, and to watching you soar.

With love and prayers always,
Mom

Table of Contents

Introduction

Motherhood. What a life-altering word. It's one of those words that can hardly even be defined. Motherhood is a concept that is rich, deep, complicated and all-encompassing. From the day you enter this ancient sisterhood, your life will never be the same. I mean, think about it...has anything in the world ever changed your life as much as becoming a mother?

No matter how many moms you know or how many little ones you have cared for; no matter how many books you've read or how many months you've spent preparing to enter into this phase of life called motherhood, it always seems to give you, and take from you, more than you could have ever imagined. Motherhood changes your life forever and surprises you every day. Believe it or not, this is still true for me after more than 24 years.

So, what was your life like before becoming a mom? What defined you? Did you earn a college degree, or even go to graduate school? Did you establish a career? Do mission work? Build a network of friends and colleagues? Earn an impressive paycheck? Maybe since having those little ones you have started to feel like you aren't that same confident, competent person anymore; like your days are just a blur of dirty dishes, dirty laundry and dirty diapers with no end in sight. And what is the point anyway? Nothing you do seems to stay done for very long.

Without a doubt, every mom can relate to those feelings. So much of what we do seems to be unappreciated, unnoticed, and undone in a matter of minutes. On our toughest days, when little ones are sick, or they can't seem to be in the same room without fighting, or we haven't had enough sleep, it's especially difficult to see the purpose behind the endless tasks that fill our days, and often our nights.

But today I'm asking you to challenge that thinking; to look at the big picture of your life and your children's lives. What if this season of your life, this intense stage of mothering little ones, could be the most challenging, important and rewarding career of your lifetime? After all, it is just a stage, and when those precious children are grown and have their own lives to lead, you will once again be able to spend your days as you choose.

But right now...today... you have a unique opportunity to influence your children and impact who they will grow up to be. Their hearts and minds, their bodies and personalities, their values and worldviews are all developing so quickly as they grow. You have an awesome,

God-given opportunity and responsibility to nurture, teach and train them in the way they should go. These are crucial days that you can never get back and they really do disappear as quickly as they came. How will you make the most of this opportunity?

Rose Kennedy said, "I looked on child rearing not only as a work of love and duty, but as a profession that was fully as interesting and challenging as any honorable profession in the world, and one that demanded the best that I could bring to it." I couldn't agree more.

So what does it mean to maximize motherhood? Maximize means "to increase as much as possible, to use in a way that will get the best results, or to make the most of something." To make the most of this season of motherhood while we can...now that is a worthy challenge.

When I first became a mother 24 years ago, I began searching for information on how to be a great mom. I became a Christian that same year, and quickly realized I had a lot to learn. A lot. So the first place I searched was God's Word. He taught me how to live a completely different life than what I had known. I also began reading lots of books by Christian authors, talking and listening to other mothers I admire and trying to learn from mistakes, both mine and others'.

Eventually I noticed that my collection of books fell neatly into six categories: faith, marriage, health, time management, money and parenting. God has shown me that if we, as mothers, focus on maximizing each of these six areas of our lives, we will be on our way to maximizing motherhood.

Of course, I haven't always succeeded at being the mom I hope to be. We all have days when we fall into bed praying that God would erase that particular day from our children's memories. We snapped at them, used words that damaged their tender spirits, and were just too depleted to give them the time and energy they deserved. We all feel like we are failing at motherhood sometimes. But I want to encourage you today that you are doing a great work! AND you are doing a great job!

The moms I mentor now are doing such a great job, but they all seem to feel so overwhelmed and exhausted. They feel as if they just can't live up to what is expected of them. But part of the problem is that they can't help comparing themselves with other moms they know on social media. Please, dear mamas, don't compare your real personal life with someone else's public persona! Anyone can post a picture-perfect moment and make it look like their life is ideal. But you know, don't you, that they still have dirty diapers and grocery store tantrums to deal with, just like you do?

Don't put too much pressure on yourself to be and do everything. You, your husband and God are the only ones who can set reasonable expectations for you. What do you need to lay down today?

What I hope to accomplish in the pages of this book is to encourage you and challenge you in small and specific ways to make the most of this amazing God-given opportunity called motherhood. I don't want you to look back 20 years from now and have regrets because you just didn't realize what a gift these years were! I know the days seem never-ending, tedious and sometimes unbearable. But please believe me when I tell you, the years will fly by and you will actually miss those little ones crawling up on your lap and begging you to read one more story.

Before you can blink you will watch them drive away in a car by themselves for the very first time. And then you will help them pack up their room and drive them to college and you will cry the whole way home. And when you do, I hope you will feel a deep sense of satisfaction and gratitude for the amazing privilege of being a mom. And I hope you will be glad that you made the most of every day you had them with you. So let's get to it...it's time to maximize motherhood.

Maximize Your Time

Day 1

"She gets up while it is still dark. She provides food for her family and portions for her servant girls."

- Proverbs 31:15

Proverbs 31 is one of my favorite chapters in the Bible. Although at first, I must admit there was a love/hate relationship between me and this perfect, godly, productive woman! It was even worse than seeing someone's perfect life on Facebook every day. While I admired her and wanted to be like her, it seemed like an unattainable goal. God still uses this ideal woman to challenge and encourage me to live my best life, and the good news is, we get to keep growing as long as we live.

This verse tells us that she gets up and busy about her work very early in the morning. Getting up early has been one of the greatest things I've done to maximize my time every day, but it hasn't always been easy. We all know how it feels to be awakened from a sound sleep by a crying baby or a sick child. Immediately, before you can even get your bearings, someone needs you. That's not a great way to start the day.

Of course, no matter how determined you are to get up before your little ones, there may still be days when they awaken early and nix your plans. But don't let that stop you from trying to establish a good morning routine. When they are on a fairly predictable schedule, begin to set your alarm for shortly before they usually get up. Even 15-30 minutes is enough of a head start to help you feel like you are ready to face the day.

Here's the key: You need to plan very carefully how you will spend these precious moments. They will set the tone for the rest of your day, so make them count!

- Begin with something you like to drink like coffee, tea, or lemon water.
- Put on some soft music or just enjoy the quiet.
- Have a special place you can go to sit and read, pray, and journal.
- Soak in the Savior's love for you, so that you will be ready to share it.
- Make a list of the most important things that need to happen that day.
- If they are still sleeping, read a few pages in an encouraging book, do some stretches, take a walk, throw in the first load of laundry, or begin

whatever tasks will help you feel like you have gotten a jump on the day.

You may notice I didn't mention spending time on your phone, computer, iPad or any electronic device. Try to discipline yourself not to let technology into your quiet morning moments. As you know, once we start scrolling, it's very easy to lose track of 30 minutes, so save the screens for later. Once you get into the habit of taking the first moments of your day to read, pray, think and prepare, you won't even mind getting up a bit earlier. Trust me, it's worth the effort.

Think and Grow:
- Do you make an effort to start your day before your children get up?
- How do you think 30 minutes of well-spent time could improve your mornings?
- What time would you need to get up to make it happen? Set your alarm now.

Prayer:
Thank you, Lord, for the example of the Proverbs 31 woman. Even though I can be intimidated by her, she serves as a godly example for me to follow. Help me to wake up

early and begin my days with you so that I will be well equipped to serve my family. Give me wisdom to plan these precious moments with thought and care and to maximize my time each day. In Jesus' name. Amen.

Thoughts...

Day 2

"Therefore, do not worry about tomorrow, for tomorrow will worry about itself. Each day has enough trouble of its own."

- Matthew 6:34

Managing our time well means making wise choices about what we do with the hours we have each day. But it also means making wise choices about what we choose NOT to do with that time. What are the time-wasters in your life? Be honest, I won't tell anyone. Do you spend hours each week scrolling through Facebook, Instagram and Twitter feeds? Are you addicted to Netflix? Most of us can identify at least one time-waster.

But have you ever thought about how much time you've spent worrying? Worry is a huge time-waster for some people. You can't be in two places at once. You cannot be fully present and engaged in living a beautiful life today if a part of you is busy worrying about what tomorrow will bring.

Each day has enough trouble of its own, but also enough joy, love, laughter, purpose and opportunity as well! Which are you looking for? Don't miss out on any of the blessings God has to offer you today because you are focused on trouble that may or may not come tomorrow. Each day is a precious, once-in-a lifetime gift, and I don't want to waste any of them on worry!

The more you begin to know God and experience his presence in your life, the more you will learn to trust him. He can handle anything that comes your way, and he is already going ahead of you to prepare the road for your journey. So the next time you're tempted to spend time worrying about the future, make the choice to trust God and fully enjoy all the blessings of today!

Think and Grow:
- What have you been worrying about lately?
- Are there other time-wasters in your life?
- What changes can you make to maximize your time?

Prayer:

Thank you, Lord, for today. Thank you for each new day you give me. Help me to see each day as the precious gift it is. Show me the time-wasters in my life and help me to take back that time and use it for a greater purpose. Give me grace to trust you with today and the future, so that I can replace worry with your peace. In Jesus' name. Amen.

Thoughts...

Day 3

"Be very careful, then, how you live - not as unwise but as wise, making the most of every opportunity, because the days are evil. Therefore, do not be foolish, but understand what the Lord's will is."

- Ephesians 5:15-17

Are you very careful how you live? Have you noticed that if you aren't careful to plan out your days, they will somehow get away from you without much to show for them? Of course, with little ones in the house, you can work hard all day and still not have completed any projects; I'm not talking about that. Caring for your children is time well spent. What I mean is that we need to plan out our days to be sure we are doing the things that are most important. And for each of us those things will be different.

We talked yesterday about time-wasters and I challenged you to look for those areas in your life. Now let's look at what will replace them. What are your goals for this week? this month? this year? Maybe you want to get in shape and lose a few pounds. Maybe this will be the year you plant a garden or learn to crochet. Or perhaps you want to spend more time reading to your children. Whatever those goals are, write them down. Don't skip this important step! It is a proven fact that writing down your goals is crucial to achieving them.

Once you have determined your goals, the next step is to determine how to go about achieving them. It's like planning a trip; your goal is the destination, but you need to map out how you will get there. Break down each goal into the smaller steps you need to accomplish. Then begin incorporating each small step into your daily schedule. You must set aside the time and make it a priority to chip away at your goals day after day, or a year from now you will look back and wonder why they didn't happen.

Find a day planner that you like and use it every day. There are countless planners and calendars to choose from, both paper and digital, but the key is to find one that works for you, and then put everything on it. Dentist appointments, kids' soccer games, time to work toward your goals, date nights with your husband, everything! In his book, "Simplify: Ten Practices to Unclutter Your Soul," pastor and author Bill Hybels says, "My schedule is far less about what I want to get done and far more about what I want to become." So decide what you want to become, and begin investing your days in that direction.

Think and Grow:
- What are three goals you would like to accomplish?
- How can you make time in your days to work toward those goals?
- Decide on a planner that works for you and begin today to use it!

Prayer:

Father, you have placed these dreams in my heart. Help me see how I can begin to make progress toward them each day. I want to become all that you have planned for me, so lead me, as I live each day, to invest my time wisely. Give me the wisdom to invest in things that matter for eternity, and the discipline to follow through until each goal is a reality. In Jesus' name. Amen.

Thoughts...

Day 4

"She watches over the affairs of her household and does not eat the bread of idleness.
                                    - Proverbs 31:27

And here we have the Proverbs 31 woman again. This woman is busy taking care of the business of her home. She is on top of things. She is not sitting around gossiping or spending hours on the internet. She knows what needs to be accomplished and she gets to work to make it happen.

Now, don't get me wrong. I'm not saying that we need to be cleaning and cooking every minute of the day! If our goal is to maximize our time, then we will make time for trips to the park, reading stories and building blanket forts. We will make space on our calendar for date nights, moms' group mornings and connecting with family members and friends. The key is to ensure that our homes are not being neglected while we are out enjoying life. And let's face it, enjoying life is a lot easier in a tidy home, with clean clothes and plenty of healthy food.

Idleness is defined as "habitually doing nothing or avoiding work." It seems to me that most mothers rarely "do nothing," but this generation of moms is tempted with so many distractions that cause us to "avoid work," even if that is not our intention. We have our cell phones with us 24 hours a day and have been conditioned to respond to every ping, buzz and beep notifying us of another like, comment or message. Meanwhile, our children need help with their lunch, the laundry needs folding and the bathroom hasn't been cleaned in weeks.

What's a mom to do? Well, what if we designated certain times of the day to sit down and reply to all those messages, rather than letting our notifications be the boss of our days? What if we set goals that need to be accomplished each day before we allow ourselves to turn on Netflix? And what if we decided that we would no longer "eat the bread of idleness"? We may just look a little more like the Proverbs 31 woman at the end of the day.

Think and Grow:
- What distractions keep you from your work throughout the day?
- What steps can you take to eliminate or contain them?
- Could you try setting aside a certain time of day to respond to messages?

Prayer:

Lord, I want to bring glory to you in everything that I do, and that includes my household responsibilities. Please show me ways that I am "eating the bread of idleness" and give me the humility to change. Help me find ways to make the most of the precious time you give me each day and not take it for granted or squander it away. I know that once a day is gone I can never get it back, and although these days can be challenging, they are priceless. In Jesus' name. Amen.

Thoughts…

Day 5

"Then Jesus said to them, 'The Sabbath was made to meet the needs of people, and not people to meet the requirements of the Sabbath.'"

- Mark 2:27

When I first started following Jesus, the concept of Sabbath was completely new to me. I grew up in a family that didn't go to church, and our family business was open seven days a week. (This was in the 1970's, long before every business was open on Sundays.) We were raised to believe that earning money and working hard were of supreme importance.

As a new Christian, I really wanted to learn about God's ways and apply them to my life, but I had so much to learn and most of it was exactly the opposite of everything I had been taught. An entire day just to rest? And do no work at all? On purpose? It sounded like a foreign language. But I loved God and trusted him enough to believe that he might just know what he was talking about.

The Bible has lots to say about the Sabbath day. Dozens of verses give rules and regulations, complete with the threat of death for breaking any of them! It can make the idea of attempting to keep the Sabbath day holy seem daunting, if not impossible. But discovering this verse changed my thinking completely. Jesus tells us that he made the Sabbath day FOR us, in order to meet our needs, not to give us a list of rules to follow. It's one of his many gifts to us.

The season of mothering little ones is an especially busy and demanding one. In fact, I quickly discovered that I could work nonstop seven days a week and still never be finished. The very next day (or hour) there will be more meals, dishes, laundry and messes to tackle.

So here is the key...if you don't intentionally take a day to rest, you won't ever get one! Of course, you will still have some things that need to be done; hungry babies and dirty diapers won't wait while you rest for a day. But you could make a big pot of soup on Saturday and just warm it up on Sunday, or have sandwiches on paper plates to make cleanup easier. You can determine from now on that you will not be doing laundry, cleaning the house or paying the bills on Sunday. How about reading a book, playing with your kids, or taking a walk or a nap instead?

What I've found over the years is that I look forward to my Sabbath day of rest so much. It's a chance for me to breathe, let go of my responsibilities and tasks and replenish myself for the week to come. And guess what...instead of losing productivity, God somehow seems to multiply my efforts so that I can accomplish more in six days than I ever did before in seven days. Hmm. Imagine that...God knows what he's talking about.

Think and Grow:
- What steps can you take to establish a Sabbath day of rest for yourself ?
- How can you incorporate Sabbath rest into your family's schedule?
- If you could choose one thing to do, just for you, what would it be? Put it on your calendar for Sunday.

Prayer:
Thank you, God, for teaching me about the Sabbath day. I know that if it was your idea, it must be a good one. Help me to accept it as the gift that you meant it to be for me, rather than viewing it as a list of rules to follow. Show me how my family can honor you and replenish our spirits by keeping one day a week holy and set apart for you. In Jesus' name. Amen.

Thoughts...

Maximize Your Faith

Day 6

"Let us not give up meeting together, as some are in the habit of doing, but let us encourage one another - and all the more as you see the Day approaching."

- Hebrews 10:25

When we think about maximizing our faith, meeting with other Christians for worship and fellowship is one of the first activities that comes to mind. If we want to follow Jesus, we need to attend church regularly, right? It seems so obvious, but have you noticed how easy it has become to skip church on any given week? I love the fact that many churches now have their services online, but maybe we are more tempted to rationalize missing church when we can say, "Oh, I'll just catch it later online." It can be an enticing alternative, especially for us introverts, but when we choose to skip services we miss out on a golden opportunity to encourage one another.

Maybe no one ever told you this before, but your church is not just for you. I hope that doesn't come as a shock to you, but when you miss church you are not the only one who misses out on a blessing. Who was at church that day that you could have blessed with a smile or a kind word? Who came through the doors of your church for the first time just looking for a friendly face? And who didn't go to church at all, because no one has invited them to go?

I know several people who haven't been to church in a long time because they can't find a place of worship that makes them happy. They don't feel comfortable, or no one said hello to them, or the pastor said something that offended them. I know these can be very real concerns, but maybe we are missing the point just a bit. A church is just like any other organization, in that it's made up of imperfect people and led by imperfect people. But that's okay because we are all there to acknowledge our flaws and tap into the Source of perfection. His power gives us the hope, strength and courage to face the challenges of this life. We can't do it in our own strength. We need him and we need each other!

So how about you? Are you in the habit of gathering at a weekly worship service? If not, I want to challenge you today to begin the process of connecting with a local church. Become part of a faith community. If not for yourself, do it for your children! They need a place where they can learn about Jesus, grow in their faith and worship the Lord. The habit of weekly worship is one of the greatest lifelong gifts you can give them.

Think and Grow:
- If you have given up meeting together in weekly worship, why?
- Ask God to show you how your family can become involved in a faith family.
- What friends or family members could you ask about attending church with them?

Prayer:

Thank you, Lord, for reminding us in your Word that meeting together for weekly worship is important to you and important for my family. We praise you that we live in a free country where we are able to worship you at many different styles and types of churches. Thank you for this opportunity to instill the habit of weekly worship into my children. In Jesus' name. Amen.

Thoughts...

Day 7

"And without faith, it is impossible to please God, because anyone who comes to Him must believe that He exists and that He rewards those who earnestly seek Him."

- Hebrews 11:6

What does the word faith mean to you? Does it mean simply that you believe that there is a God? That you believe Jesus died on the cross to forgive your sins and take you to heaven with him someday? This verse takes faith a bit deeper to discover what kind of faith pleases God. And isn't that the kind of faith we want to have? Isn't that the kind of faith we want to teach to our children?

Oh how I love this verse. It gives us such a clear picture of the type of Father our God longs to be to us. He is a God who not only exists, but he REWARDS those who earnestly seek him. And when we believe that about him, it pleases him. And it stands to reason that if we believe that he rewards those who earnestly seek him, we will want to be one of those seekers! We will be motivated to seek him in all that we do and we will teach our children, by word and by example, to seek him too.

So what if you aren't there yet in your faith journey? What if you have only a tiny bit of faith? Maybe you or your child believes that God is real, but haven't learned to trust him with everything in your life or truly believe in his goodness. How do we grow our faith? There are lots of ways, but three of the best I have discovered are:

1. Read the history of God's faithfulness in the Bible and other Christian books.
2. Listen to Christian music and songs of faith.
3. Spend time with people who have big faith.

Even in this busy season of your life, you can find ways to incorporate these three habits into your life. Play Christian music in the kitchen, in the car and when you're folding laundry. Make time to read a few pages of the Bible and other Christian literature before the babies wake up in the morning, while they are napping or after they are in bed at night. And search for friends and mentors whose faith you admire. Join a moms' group at your church, become part of a life group or an online group. And most importantly, pray and ask God to grow your faith. That's a prayer he will be happy to answer.

Think and Grow:
- How do you define faith?
- Do you believe God rewards those who earnestly seek him?
- What steps can you take to actively grow your faith and help your children grow theirs as well?

Prayer:
Loving God, thank you so much for the many truths in your Word. I'm thrilled to discover that you want to reward me when I earnestly seek you! Please help me to grow my faith in you and in your character. Help my children to also grow into people of strong faith. I realize that there is no better time than now to get started growing my faith. "I do believe, but help me overcome my unbelief!" (Mark 9:24) In Jesus' name. Amen.

Thoughts...

Day 8

"Do not be anxious about anything, but in everything, by prayer and petition, with thanksgiving, present your requests to God. And the peace of God, which transcends all understanding, will guard your hearts and your minds in Christ Jesus."

- Philippians 4:6-7

Is there anything on Earth that gives us more cause to "be anxious" than motherhood? The baby has a fever. Your toddler has learned the word "no." Someone decided it's time for your five-year-old to spend all day at kindergarten. The teenager just got his driver's license. And on it goes. Two of my children are now in their twenties and I still have opportunities to be anxious on a daily basis. But God shows us a better way.

Any time God says "do not" to us it means that this particular thing is under our control. We have the choice to do it or to not do it. "Do not be anxious." He's telling us that whether or not we become anxious is our choice, and he wants us to choose wisely. Easier said than done, right? But thankfully, this verse even tells us how to avoid being anxious.

"But in everything...present your requests to God." Prayer can be the solution for our anxiety. When we come to God in prayer with thanksgiving and present our requests to him, "the peace of God, which transcends all understanding," comes over us and invites us to lay down those anxious feelings. Notice there is no promise that God will change our circumstances, or answer our prayers the way we want him to, but what will change is how we feel on the inside. We can choose to trade our anxious thoughts for peaceful ones when we bring everything to God in prayer.

Just a note here that I'm not referring to, or in any way downplaying the type of anxiety that has been diagnosed and needs to be treated by a physician. In that case, prayer may be only a part of your plan.

Try it, my friend...it really works. And the funny part is you can't even explain why it works. (I guess that's the "transcends understanding" part.) Little by little, as you practice learning how to give God your anxious moments and allow him to replace them with his peace, you will find that things that once made you anxious just don't anymore. What freedom! I want that peace guarding my heart and mind...how about you?

Think and Grow:
- What circumstances are making you anxious today?
- How do you feel about the idea that you can choose not to be anxious?
- Begin spending time daily taking your anxious thoughts to God and asking him to trade them for his perfect peace.

Prayer:
Gracious Father, thank you for this admonition to "not be anxious about anything." I confess that I often believe that I am at the mercy of my circumstances. If things go wrong, I get stressed out. Help me to cultivate a new habit of praying to you at the first sign of an anxious thought, and grant me your peace that transcends my understanding as well as my circumstances. Thank you. In Jesus' name. Amen.

Thoughts...

Day 9

"All Scripture is God-breathed and is useful for teaching, rebuking, correcting and training in righteousness, so that the man of God may be thoroughly equipped for every good work."
                                        - 2 Timothy 3:16-17

As a woman of God, I surely want to be equipped for every good work, don't you? Each day as we care for our families and meet their never-ending needs, we wonder if we have enough to give. In this overwhelming season, it seems that the demands on our time and energy are infinite, and there are situations that are beyond our capacity to understand. What is the best way to deal with an infant who has colic, a toddler who throws temper tantrums or a teen who has chosen the wrong group of friends? When we've done what we know to do and it isn't working, where do we turn? This verse makes it clear. We can turn to the Scripture, the God-breathed book that has all the answers.

When I started following Jesus, one of the things I did first was to read my Bible, cover to cover. Yes, it took a long time, but it was important for me to see how it all fit together. And I still read God's Word every day. Knowing that God has breathed every word of the Bible to teach me, correct me and train me gives me the motivation I need to dig in!

When you start reading your Bible daily, you will be astounded at the little nuggets of wisdom you find day by day. They are better than nuggets of gold.

If you already have a habit of reading your Bible daily, great! If not, I have an idea that might help you develop this life-changing habit. Find or create a special place in your house where you will go to read your Bible every day. Choose a space that has a comfortable chair, a source of light, and a place to keep the things you'll need. Then collect your Bible, a journal, devotional books, pens, a highlighter, tissues, bookmarks and anything else you think you may need. I also have a cd player, lip balm, a nail file and some hand lotion so I don't need to keep jumping up. Coasters are good too.

Every morning when I wake up, I get a cup of tea or a glass of water and head straight to my comfy chair. There's no better way to start your day than by reading God's word, praying, and writing down a few things that you are learning. And it all starts with creating a warm, inviting place. Try it...make it a habit and it will change your life.

Think and Grow:
- Have you formed the habit of reading your Bible every day?
- Create a welcoming space that you look forward to spending time in each day.
- Decide on a Bible reading plan and begin today.

Prayer:

Thank you, Lord, for breathing your life into every word of the Bible. You know that we need the teaching, rebuking, correcting and training in righteousness that your Word provides. Help me to develop a habit of starting each day with this perfect training. Help me to create a beautiful, inviting place of my own to meet with you each day, and then give me the strength I need to follow through and use it. I believe that you will use this habit to change my life. In Jesus' name. Amen.

Thoughts...

Day 10

"Just as the body is dead without breath, so also faith is dead without good works."
                              - James 2:26

Make no mistake, we are saved by faith alone. If we believe that Jesus died on the cross to carry the weight of our sins, and we confess that he is the Lord of our lives, we have been saved and will spend eternity in heaven with him. So we do not need to do "good works" in order to make God love us, or to get to heaven. However, if we want our faith to be alive and well and able to draw others to him, we also need to have good works in our lives.

You may be thinking, "What? Now I have to find time to go work in a soup kitchen or teach Sunday school? I barely had time to brush my teeth yesterday!" Relax, it's easier than you think. "Good works" are just all the ways we serve the Lord by serving others. So when you helped your little boy tie his shoes for the fifteenth time today, that was "good works". When you made your husband's favorite dinner for him, that was too. Each time you show God's love to your family, neighbors, friends or the clerk at the grocery store, you are doing good works. Simply go about your day with the attitude, "How can I show God's love to those around me today?" and you will be on the right track.

Of course, there is a place for more formal serving experiences too. Over the years, our family has delivered meals from the Rescue Mission on Thanksgiving, helped many single moms, volunteered at our local church in countless ways, and served on mission trips around the world.

But there is a time and a season for everything. Right now, if you are a full-time mommy with little ones at home, every day of your life is about serving. And make no mistake, showing God's love to your family is every bit as valuable as volunteering in any other ministry.

If you have a strong desire to give more to your community, ask God if he has other opportunities in mind for you, then be open to whatever he shows you. And include your children in your good works whenever possible. What a wonderful way to spend time as a family.

Think and Grow:
- What does the term "good works" mean to you?
- Ask yourself, "How can I show God's love to those around me today?"

- Begin asking God what good works he may have in mind for you and your family.

Prayer:

Father God, thank you for providing each of us with a way to spend eternity with you. I'm so thankful that because I have trusted Jesus as my Savior, I know that one day I will be in heaven. You don't ask me to do anything else to secure my position or earn your love. And yet, you ask me to go out into my world and share your love with others. Help me to be more aware of opportunities to serve others each day. In Jesus' name. Amen.

Thoughts...

Maximize Your Money

Day 11

"And this same God who takes care of me will supply all your needs from his glorious riches, which have been given to us in Christ Jesus."
- Philippians 4:19

Just read that verse one more time and think about it for a minute. The God of the universe, the one who owns the cattle on a thousand hills, the Creator of every good thing, will supply all your needs. That, my friend, is incredible news! When the paycheck doesn't seem like it will last as long as the bills, when that unexpected repair bill throws the budget off again, when your daughter needs braces, (they cost HOW MUCH??) you can look back at this verse and thank God that he will continue to supply all your needs out of HIS glorious riches, not out of your earthly bank account.

Do we live like we truly believe this awesome promise? If we believe and trust that God will meet all our needs, how will that affect the way we live our daily lives? Maybe we would refrain from buying things we think we need right now with money we don't have yet. You know, like using a credit card or consumer loan to gather more stuff. Maybe we would actually stop and turn to God when we have a true need and then wait expectantly for him to meet it. And when he came through, like only he could, we would marvel at his creativity, generosity and overwhelming love and care for us and we would fall in love with him all over again.

I love to turn to God in these "impossible" situations and just wait for him to show off. I can remember so many times over the years when he provided for our family in amazing ways. A few years ago, we were going on vacation, and took our van to get an oil change and just have it checked out for safety purposes. Well, we discovered that it would have cost more to fix everything wrong with that van than it was actually worth. And so we needed to find a new van. In four days. With only $4,000 in our savings account. (We have been living without debt for many years in obedience to God, so a car loan was not an option for us.)

Well, this was the perfect opportunity for God to show us how it's done. When we were finally on our way to the beach, all six of us and our luggage, headed on a ten-hour drive, we marveled at how our Father had supplied our need once again. And when I looked up our "new" van on Kelley Blue Book, I discovered that it was actually worth more than twice what we paid for it. Yep, that's my Jesus. He always comes through.

Think and Grow:
- Do you really believe that God will supply all your needs?
- Have you seen your Father provide something for you in an amazing way?
- Next time you have a need, ask Him to provide and watch what happens.

Prayer:
Father, thank you for this promise that you will supply all my needs according to your glorious riches. Help me learn to really trust and believe that your promises are true. Show me opportunities to rely on you instead of pulling out the credit card. I invite you to help me grow my faith by learning to trust you, wait on you and give you opportunities to work in my life. In Jesus' name. Amen.

Thoughts...

Day 12

"'Bring all the tithes into the storehouse so there will be enough food in my Temple. If you do,' says the lord of Heaven's Armies, 'I will open the windows of heaven for you. I will pour out a blessing so great you won't have enough room to take it in! Try it! Put me to the test!'"

- Malachi 3:10

Well, this sounds like the kind of experiment I would really enjoy, how about you? When the God of Heaven's Armies says he will pour out a blessing so great I won't even be able to take it in, I'm game to try it! So what exactly is the tithe, anyway? Simply put, it is giving the first 10% of your income to God. That can sound a bit ridiculous when you think about it. God doesn't need our money. He is the Creator of the universe, and he owns it all. So why would He ask us to give him the first tenth of our income? Because we need to learn how to let go of it. We need to learn how to have money without it having us.

When we give the first 10% of our paycheck to the church, before we think about what we'd like to buy with it, before we store it up in investments for our security, even before we pay our bills, we learn. We learn that God is faithful and we can trust him to meet our needs. We learn that true security comes from our relationship with our Creator, and not from a bank account. And we learn that a rich, full, meaningful life comes from putting obedience to God and the needs of others before our own desires. That's why he asks us to give.

When we learned about tithing as young parents, there was absolutely no room in our budget for giving. In fact, because of some unfortunate financial decisions, we were actually going backwards every month. So we made some changes. We sold the more costly house we were living in and moved into one much more suited to our family and our budget. That allowed us to begin tithing, and even giving above that when opportunities came along. We have put God to the test on this and brought our tithes to the church first, even when we couldn't see how our other bills would be paid. And guess what? He has been faithful. We have always been blessed with more than enough, financially and otherwise.

I know it can seem scary at first, but don't take my word for it, take God at his word and put him to the test! You might just be blessed beyond what you can imagine. Help your children become tithers from the very beginning, too. When they receive an allowance or money for small jobs, they can begin to give the first 10% to God and it will become a lifelong habit.

Think and Grow:
- Is your family currently tithing?
- What hesitations do you have about giving before paying other expenses?
- Are you willing to take God at his word and put him to the test?

Prayer:
Father, thank you for all the wisdom in the Bible. Thank you for teaching me about everything in life, including money management. Even though I may be apprehensive about giving 10% right off the top of our income, I trust you and I can't wait to see how you will open the windows of heaven for me and my family as we obey you. Give us the courage to make whatever changes may be needed. In Jesus' name. Amen.

Thoughts...

Day 13

"Owe nothing to anyone - except for your obligation to love one another..."
                                              - Romans 13:8

"Just as the rich rule the poor, so the borrower is servant to the lender."
                                              - Proverbs 22:7

You probably knew this day was coming. We're talking about how to maximize your money from a biblical perspective, so we need to discuss the dreaded topic of debt. If you are in debt then you already know that the borrower is servant to the lender. You (and/or your husband) go to work and serve each day to pay back your lenders. It seems that everyone is in the same boat.

The world we live in today would like us to think that debt is inevitable. Every commercial tries to convince you that you need something newer, bigger, and better, regardless of your ability to pay for it. Credit cards, car loans, mortgages, second and third mortgages, reverse mortgages, and buy-now-pay-later promotions all make it possible for us to own so much more than we can really afford.

Debt can be like a snowball. It starts out innocently enough, with a car loan or some furniture bought on credit. But then an unexpected car repair or medical bill comes along and suddenly you can no longer afford to pay the monthly payments on all your debt. This results in the very stressful situation in which every month you are putting more and more of your living expenses on credit cards in order to make ends meet. Suddenly your financial situation feels helpless, hopeless and out of control. And of course, the resulting stress spells disaster for your health and relationships, especially your marriage.

So the best advice is found in Romans 13:8... "Owe no man anything." In other words, if you don't have debt, great! Keep it that way. Live within your means, save for a rainy day and always try to expect those unexpected expenses.

But if it's too late for that and your family already has a pile of debt, get some help. Dave Ramsey has a great plan for dealing with debt in his books and on his website, www.daveramsey.com

Above all, pray and seek God's wisdom in your financial situation. There may be no quick fix, but the peace of mind you gain from living debt-free will be worth any effort it takes to get there.

Think and Grow:
- How has consumer debt impacted your life, marriage and family life?
- Are you and your husband in agreement about avoiding debt?
- What steps can you take to begin eliminating debt from your life?

Prayer:
Lord, I'm constantly amazed by the depth of wisdom found in your Word. If only we would heed that wisdom more often, we could avoid so much of the trouble in our lives. Thank you for your clear warnings about avoiding debt. I confess that I haven't always wanted to accept that your ways are best. I've wanted to jump ahead of you and get things for myself that I wasn't ready to pay for. Please forgive me for disregarding your wise counsel and help me dig out of the mess I've made. Guide me to make wise decisions from this day forward. In Jesus' name. Amen.

Thoughts…

Day 14

"She sees that her trading is profitable, and her lamp does not go out at night."
                                    - Proverbs 31:18

This verse really hits home for me. My husband is the hardest working man I know, and yet our family has always been on a tight budget. We avoid debt and work hard to live within our means. Over the years I have learned lots of ways to see that my trading is profitable, mostly out of necessity. Of course, in today's economy, we don't really trade goods anymore, we trade our hard-earned dollars for the things our family needs. After we give the first 10% to the church and pay the monthly bills, how much is left for food, clothing, household items, gifts, etc? For us it never seemed to work out on paper. We were depending on God to make our ends meet, and he always did. So when we needed to shop for something I had to get creative.

One great way to see that your trading is profitable is to participate in yard sales. Each year we would have a big yard sale to clean out everything that our kids had outgrown that year. Not just clothing, but toys, books, even furniture and other household items. We would then use the money we earned to shop at yard sales all summer, searching for new treasures. My book collection has been built mostly from yard sales. I've also found lots of new and like-new Christmas gifts, including an American Girl doll for $1.00. It's also a fun way to spend a Saturday morning. My husband and I will often consider that our date for the week. Of course, much of what you find at these sales is just other people's junk, but when you find that one perfect item, it's worth all the searching. And it is certainly profitable trading.

Another place where you can save lots of money is the grocery bill. Between discount grocery stores, coupons, weekly sales and local farmers markets, there are so many opportunities to cut expenses. Use what's in season, cook from scratch, buy in bulk, and make good use of any leftovers to maximize your grocery budget. I did an experiment earlier this year to see how low I could cut our food bill, and for three months I fed our family of six (and guests) for $50.00 a week. It isn't easy, but it is possible.

I'm sure you can think of lots of other ways to be sure that your trading is profitable. I have cut our family's hair for years, earned free vacations using credit card points, used store coupons and clearance sales, and even made lots of gifts to give at the holidays. The bottom line is, the more value you can get for your hard-earned dollar, the more you will have left over to save, invest, pay down debt or give when a need arises. It pays to be a good steward of our resources, and our children learn from our example.

Think and Grow:
- Can you think of areas in your budget where your trading could be more profitable?
- If you were to cut your spending, what could you do with those savings?
- Consider gathering items for a yard sale and put a date on the calendar.

Prayer:
Father, thank you for reminding me to be a good steward of the resources you have entrusted to my family. I want to honor you in everything, including our spending, saving and giving. Show me ways to maximize each paycheck and give me the wisdom and self-control to follow through, for your glory. In Jesus' name. Amen.

Thoughts…

Day 15

"Dishonest money dwindles away, but whoever gathers money little by little makes it grow."
- Proverbs 13:11

Have you ever heard the story of someone who has won the lottery? I was shocked to hear that almost without fail, lottery winners eventually end up completely broke. How can that be? We see them standing there with their big checks and even bigger smiles, believing that all their troubles are now behind them. We would all love to trade places with them at that moment. I mean, after all, who hasn't thought that a big sum of money would solve all of our problems?

We can see the same thing happen with people who suddenly inherit a large sum of money, or even actors and athletes who rise to sudden fame and fortune only to come crashing down a few years later. "Dishonest money dwindles away...." We have seen it happen time and time again. Even if the person has honestly earned the money, so much wealth all at once seems too much to handle.

The wisdom in this verse tells us that a much better idea is to gather, or save money little by little and make it grow. If you (or your husband) have a 401k or an IRA you are already following this advice. Or maybe you have a savings account to which you contribute on a regular basis so you will have money for those unexpected emergencies. If not, do what it takes to get an automatic saving and investing plan in place right away. It's best if it can come right out of your paycheck, before taxes, so you won't even miss it. Especially if your employer offers to match some part of your contribution, don't let another week go by without taking advantage of that opportunity.

The mistake most of us make is that we decide to save whatever is left after all the bills are paid. But here's the thing... there never seems to be anything left over. It's a strange phenomenon, but we somehow manage to spend whatever is available to spend. Think about it, the last time you got a raise, did it change your life? Unless you were intentional about telling that money where to go, it probably just got absorbed into your spending habits and after a while it was like the raise never even happened.

The secret to gathering money little by little is saving right off the top, before it even goes into your bank account. Make it automatic so you don't need to think about it. Pay yourself first, as the saying goes. This is so important to your future financial independence and the well-being of your family. And it's easier than you think.

Think and Grow:

- Are you in the habit of gathering money, little by little to make it grow?
- How would having a saving and investment plan change your life?
- Take the necessary steps today. Your family will thank you.

Prayer:

Dear God, I'm amazed at your wisdom. All throughout the Bible, you have scattered sound advice for our daily lives. You knew that winning the lottery would never solve our problems, but the discipline of hard work and consistent saving would one day give us financial peace and independence. Guide me through the steps I need to take next. In Jesus' name. Amen.

Thoughts…

Maximize Your Health

Day 16

"Do you not know that your bodies are temples of the Holy Spirit, who is in you, whom you have received from God? You are not your own; you were bought at a price. Therefore honor God with your bodies."

- 1 Corinthians 6:19-20

As we begin our look into how we can maximize our health, let's acknowledge that this is a difficult area for many of us. Especially during the season of pregnancy, childbirth and caring for young children, the easiest thing to do is forget about taking care of ourselves. Forget about exercise (who has time or energy for that anyway?). Forget about healthy food (processed snacks and fast foods are much easier and quicker). And forget about sleep (the babies take care of this one for us).

Look, I've been there and I fully understand "survival mode." But read today's verse again. Your body is a temple of the Holy Spirit. God himself lives inside you if you have accepted him as your Lord and Savior. So you have been bought with a high price, the blood of Jesus, and you are no longer your own. And that, dear sisters, is why we must strive to honor God with our bodies.

I'm not trying to put more demands on you than you already have, just hoping to help you take small steps in a healthier direction. When you are tempted to reach for that next soda, choose a glass of water with lemon instead. Instead of eating your preschooler's leftovers, make a healthy lunch for yourself. And if by some miracle all the children take a nap at the same time, lie down and rest your weary self! Maybe your hubby or your mom or a friend would even stay with your little ones so you could take a walk around the neighborhood or go to the gym.

You spend all day and half the night caring for your family, but you deserve to take better care of YOU too. And what happens if you don't? Well, you may be able to continue on that path for a while, but eventually it will catch up with you. That dreaded baby weight will be harder to shake, you will be worn out and, dare I say it, maybe even a little bit grumpy. Well, not you, but I've heard that can happen to some people who don't take care of themselves.

Honestly, I'm sure you've heard this before, but in case you need a little reminder today, taking care of yourself is so important. People are counting on you. Your family needs you every day, and they need you to be healthy, happy and strong. So put yourself back on your to-do list today. It is not selfish to invest time and energy in your own self-care. You will be honoring God and blessing your family at the same time.

Think and Grow:
- Would you say you are honoring God with your body?
- Are you starting to feel the negative effects of neglecting yourself?
- What steps can you take this week to begin taking care of your temple?

Prayer:
Father, thank you for reminding me that I honor you when I care for myself. The demands on my time and energy feel so overwhelming at times, and I can easily put myself and my health at the bottom of my priority list. Please show me practical ways to begin caring for myself and help me to follow through. I want to honor you and give my family the best of me. In Jesus' name. Amen.

Thoughts…

Day 17

"Please test your servants for ten days: Give us nothing but vegetables to eat and water to drink. At the end of the ten days they looked healthier and better nourished than any of the young men who ate the royal food."
                                                    - Daniel 1:12,15

As I get older, I am learning each day how important it is to be selective about what we put into our bodies. When I'm intentionally eating well, drinking lots of water and using high quality supplements*, I feel better, have much more energy, and my weight is stable. But just let me spend a few days eating junk and I can really tell the difference.

My son is 18 years old, and despite my best efforts, he lives on fast food, junk food and Mountain Dew. Unfortunately, he's at the age where if he doesn't like the healthy meal I've cooked for dinner, he just goes out to get a burger or a pizza. And he never gains an ounce, except muscle. Rude.

When I think about it, I probably did the same thing at his age. But oh my, I cannot get away with that now! And, in a way, I'm glad I can't, because it causes me to be intentional about my nutrition. Don't you love this story from the book of Daniel? The other young men who ate the king's royal food and drank his wine didn't look as healthy at the end of ten days as Daniel and his friends who refused to defile themselves with that food and consumed only vegetables and water. The next verse goes on to say that the guards proceeded to put all the men on Daniel's diet! I bet that made him Mr. Popular. But I digress…

Now, don't get me wrong, I'm not suggesting that you should eat nothing but vegetables, but it stands to reason that the more we eat food as God created it, the healthier our bodies will be. It can be such a challenge to eat only whole foods with so many packaged and fast food options to choose from. But you will be doing yourself and your family a great favor by choosing healthy, wholesome options when you shop, cook and serve meals and snacks.

Again, the best way to make big changes is to start with small steps. Trade in those sodas for water, snack on fruit, nuts and veggies with dip made from Greek yogurt, and limit fast food stops by planning ahead to cook dinners at home. The crock pot is a wonderful tool for busy moms. Just a few go-to recipes can make a huge difference in your life.

Over the years I've discovered that if I can shop wisely, that's half the battle. If you go to the grocery store armed with a menu plan and detailed list and then stick to it, your healthy eating plan will be well under way.

Think and Grow:
- Does your family eat mostly food the way God made it?
- What are you making for dinner tonight?
- Begin to plan ahead for your next grocery shopping trip.

Prayer:
God, thank you for the story of Daniel and his friends. I admire the courage and self-control they had over what they put into their bodies. Today it takes just as much courage and self-control for me and my family to stay committed to eating healthy whole foods. Temptation is everywhere in the form of rich, sugary, processed and fast food treats. Help us as we make the changes to our diet that will bring honor to you. In Jesus' name. Amen.

Thoughts…

Day 18

"She sets about her work vigorously; her arms are strong for her tasks."
                                        - Proverbs 31:17

When Proverbs 31 was written, a woman with a family to care for would have had a lot of physical work to do each and every day just to provide for their basic needs. This verse from our favorite chapter about the virtuous wife tells us that she is strong, and a hard worker. Of course, times have changed and we now have washing machines, dryers, dishwashers, cars, Amazon, running water and dozens of other amenities that make our daily work much less physically demanding. But part of honoring God with our bodies is still keeping ourselves strong, fit and energetic so that we can vigorously go about the work He gives us.

Enter another modern invention...the gym. Joining a gym may be a great solution if you are looking to get or stay in shape. Some even have child care so that you can get an hour to yourself during the day to exercise. If that isn't a good option for you right now, you can find exercise equipment and workout DVDs for sale online or at yard sales so you can work out at home. You can find just about any type of workout online too.

Even if you head outside while the kids spend some time with dad and walk, bike or run for half an hour, it will make a world of difference in your energy, fitness level and outlook. Of course, you can always put the baby in the stroller and head out to the playground together. However you get your exercise, just be sure to get it in! Physical activity is just so important for our overall health and well being. And in this digital age we need to be even more intentional about making it a part of the daily routine for our families.

One thing that has been proven to be life-changing for many women is to include strength training activity two to three days a week. No matter what your age or fitness level, you can benefit from muscle building exercises. The muscle you create will burn calories for you all day long and increase your strength and stamina, not to mention adding definition to your shape.

Start slowly, but start somewhere and keep your arms strong for your tasks. Ten years from now, you'll be glad you did. Like any other positive habit you want to build, planning is key. Decide when, where and how you will get in your workouts this week and then schedule them into your planner. No one ever drifted into excellence. It is always intentional.

Think and Grow:
- Would you say that you go about your work vigorously?
- Is your body as strong as you would like it to be?
- What steps can you take today to begin an exercise routine?

Prayer:
Father, thank you once again for the example of the Proverbs 31 woman. Even though she can be intimidating, I want to continually strive to be that wife of noble character that your word describes. I want to be physically strong so that I can go about my work vigorously throughout my lifetime. God, show me how I can begin to prioritize fitness into my everyday life, not only for my own strength, but as an example for my children as well. They deserve a strong, fit mama who can keep up with them for years to come! In Jesus' name. Amen.

Thoughts…

Day 19

"In peace I will lie down and sleep, for you alone, Lord, make me dwell in safety."
                                    - Psalm 4:8

    Ah sleep. Do you remember what sleeping was like before you became a mother? You probably didn't think much about it, because it wasn't an issue. You just went to bed whenever your day was finished and you were tired, then you slept until it was time to get up. Or, if it was the weekend and you wanted to sleep in, you could sleep until you wanted to get up.

    But then it happened...that tiny baby was born and all of a sudden you were on call 24/7 for feedings, diaper changes, and other assorted needs. And sleep, as you knew it, became a distant memory. Every few hours you would wake up, care for that precious little one, then collapse back in bed for another short nap. But somehow, when morning arrived and it was time to start your day, you didn't feel like you were ready to bounce out of bed. That interrupted sleep is just not the same, even if you add up the hours and think it should be enough.

    Eventually, and mercifully, the baby begins to sleep through the night, allowing you the same opportunity. But then, the temptation to use those evening hours for other activities becomes an issue. What do you like to do when the kids are finally down for the night? Catch up on your latest Netflix series? Scroll through various social media sites? Clean up the house and catch up on the laundry?

Whatever you do, set a time limit for yourself and be sure to wind down and get to bed in time for a solid night of sleep. A good rule of thumb would be to count backwards eight hours from the time you intend to wake up in the morning. Then plan to be in bed half an hour before that to give yourself time to fall asleep. The goal would be to wake up a few minutes before your kiddos to begin your day with a sense of peace.

Of course, there will always be times when your children need you during the night. Nightmares, illness, and trouble falling asleep are common threats to your eight hours. Now that our kids are older, they often wake us up coming in late at night or having fun with their friends a little too loudly in the house, so I guess there's always something. On those occasions, give yourself permission to catch a nap in the afternoon while your children sleep, or maybe Dad could take care of bedtime so you can turn in early. Good sleep is so important to our overall health. It is worth whatever sacrifices we need to make to keep it high on the priority list.

Think and Grow:
- What is the biggest threat to your sleep at this stage of life?
- How much sleep do you need to feel fully rested? Are you getting it?
- What steps can you take today to be sure you are getting the sleep your body needs?

Prayer:
Father, thank you for creating our bodies to need sleep. Help me to realize how critical sleep is to my overall health and well-being and treat it as a high priority. Give me wisdom to see how I can change my daily habits and routines in order to give my body plenty of time for sleep each night. And on the days when I haven't gotten enough sleep the night before, show me how I can make time for a power nap, because I realize that decision could change the course of the rest of the day for my family. In Jesus' name. Amen.

Thoughts…

Day 20

"A cheerful heart is good medicine, but a crushed spirit dries up the bones."
                                                    - Proverbs 17:22

We can't conclude our discussion on maximizing our health without a look at the leading cause of illness in our country. By now I'm sure you know, either from hearing it on the news or by experiencing it in your own life, that I'm referring to stress. Stress affects each one of us to one degree or another, and it can come from good and bad events or situations in our lives. Some degree of stress is inevitable, and can even be a good thing. But when our stress level remains elevated for a long period of time, that's when it can start adversely affecting our health. The key is to learn how to manage our stress level so that it doesn't get out of hand. Easier said than done, right?

Stressful situations arise in life that we can't control. Illness, job loss, natural disasters and sin (our own and that of others) can all cause anxiety on any given day. Even wonderful life changes like getting married, moving to a new house or having a baby can bring a huge amount of (good) stress.

But there are many avoidable causes of stress in our way of life today that we need to consider. For example, does your calendar, planner, to-do list or daily schedule make you want to cry? Do you have so much to do each day that you know there's no way you can possibly do it all? At the risk of sounding a bit sarcastic...who put those things on your agenda?

So many people I know, especially moms, are running around frantically from one activity to another with no time to even sit down and eat dinner with their families. I understand that these can be good activities, even church commitments in many cases, but what are you willing to sacrifice for some peace in your life? If you recognize that stress is a problem for you, begin by looking at your commitments and ask God which things are truly a priority in this stage of life. Then have the courage to gracefully step away from everything else.

Another thing that adds to our stress level is clutter. Even if you don't realize it, walking past piles of papers, dirty laundry (or even clean laundry waiting to be folded) or a really messy closet can drain your energy and add to your overall stress level. Tackle one of those projects and feel the difference it makes!

And what are you doing for fun? Don't forget, one of the best ways to combat stress is to play, laugh and have fun! Think of fun as something that deserves a spot on your planner each day. Streamline your schedule, chip away at those nagging household messes and plan play dates for mom. Now that's a recipe for successful stress management.

Think and Grow:
- What keeps your heart from being cheerful?
- Do you need to declutter your house and/or your schedule?
- When was the last time you planned for some fun in your life?

Prayer:
Thank you, Lord, for reminding me that a cheerful heart is good medicine. I know that in this world we will have trouble, but give me wisdom to know when I'm bringing trouble on myself, and the courage to change that. Show me today some steps I can take to eliminate extra commitments and clutter. Help me remember that my children aren't the only ones in the family who need to unwind, play and laugh on a regular basis. Thank you for your love and care. In Jesus' name. Amen

Thoughts…

Maximize Your Motherhood

Day 21

"Come to me, all you who are weary and burdened, and I will give you rest. Take my yoke upon you and learn from me, for I am gentle and humble in heart, and you will find rest for your souls. For my yoke is easy and my burden is light."

- Matthew 11:28-30

Does motherhood ever make you feel weary? No? Just me then? There were times when my children were younger (and even as they grew older) when I felt like I simply could not go on. This parenting gig just isn't what it looked like in the brochure. It demands more of you than you think you can give. And that's why I just love today's verses.

Picture a yoke built for two oxen to carry, side by side, bearing the weight together. Then picture this parenting life with you (and your husband) on one side of the yoke and Jesus on the other. Except, instead of the crushing weight of a yoke too heavy to bear, Jesus tells us that his yoke is easy and his burden is light. And so we can find rest for our souls. Doesn't that sound like the best news ever?

So how does this play out in our everyday lives? First we need to change the way we think about motherhood and the pressure we put on ourselves. In fact, parenting is too big a job for us to handle on our own, and that's why Jesus instructs us to share it with him. Not just parenting, but all of life's burdens as well. When we realize that Jesus already has a plan for our children and that he wants to walk with us and with them through every day, it changes our perspective.

Ultimately, we are not 100% responsible for, or in control of, their lives, or even our own. We don't know what the future holds, but he does. That realization frees us to simply move forward one step at a time, turning to him for guidance and trusting him with the outcome. We are then free to enjoy our children and give them our best each day.

What does it mean to find rest for your soul? I love that phrase, because even if we can't put it into words, we have all experienced times when our soul was at rest, and times when it was in turmoil. Think of a time when your soul was not at rest. What an awful feeling. You can't eat, or maybe can't stop eating, have trouble falling asleep, and no matter what else you do to distract yourself you just can't find peace inside yourself.

The next time you feel that way, remember the words of Jesus, "Come to me all who are weary and burdened and I will give you rest." Even if our days are filled with activity during the busy years of parenting, our souls can be at rest if we lean on him, and allow him to help bear our burdens.

Think and Grow:
- Is anything about motherhood making you feel weary right now?
- Does your soul crave a feeling of peace and rest?
- How can you begin to allow Jesus to carry more of your load?

Prayer:
Father, thank you for this reminder that you don't expect me to carry the burdens of this life alone. Being a good mother is so important to me and yet I fall short of my own expectations on a daily basis. Help me to really grasp the fact that I am not responsible for everything in my child's future. As I come to you with my inadequacies, help me to find rest for my soul. That is really the most important rest there is. In Jesus' name. Amen.

Thoughts…

Day 22

"Fix these words of mine in your hearts and minds; tie them as symbols on your hands and bind them on your foreheads. Teach them to your children, talking about them when you sit at home and when you walk along the road, when you lie down and when you get up."

- Deuteronomy 11:18-19

As parents, we have the opportunity and the responsibility to teach our children countless facts, skills, values and ideas about the world in which we live. When we think about how helpless a new baby is when he first becomes a part of our family, the task of helping him grow into an independent, productive adult can be completely overwhelming. So much to learn, where do we begin?

One of the most important areas I wanted to help nurture and develop in my children was their relationship with Jesus. I knew that I wouldn't be able to make all their decisions for them or be able to help them out of every tough situation. I also realized that while I tried to give the best guidance possible, even moms don't know everything. So I wanted them to draw close to the one who does.

The first thing I realized was "You can't teach what you don't know." Since I only began following Christ after becoming a mom, I had a lot to learn! So spending time at church, in Bible study, and reading good Christian books became a high priority for me. I also took the children to Sunday school and Wednesday evening programs, as well as special events like Vacation Bible School and camp meetings. Surrounding yourself and your family with good Biblical teaching and like-minded families is a great place to start. But as today's verses remind us, teaching our children to follow God is a daily way of life. They will learn most of their values and habits from what we do and say and practice every day.

As part of our homeschool day, we had family devotions in the mornings. Each child had his or her own Bible, appropriate for their age and reading level. As they grew, they were encouraged to have their own private devotional times. And we always took turns praying aloud for each other and before meals. When something difficult was happening we would turn to God for wisdom, guidance and comfort. And when anything wonderful happened we remembered to thank God from whom all blessings flow.

Each day brings opportunities and teaching moments if we are just aware of God's activity in our lives as we sit at home, walk along the road, when we lie down and get up. So talk to your children about God and talk to God about your children. Learn about him together and treat him like a member of your family. As they grow up, your children will naturally include God in their lives because he's been there from the beginning. And that's the most precious gift you could ever give them.

Think and Grow:
- Does your everyday life with your children include talking about and to God?
- Would you agree that teaching your children to know, love, and trust God is a top priority?
- What steps can you take toward that goal?

Prayer:
Thank you, God, for the privilege of walking together with you and my family each day. Help me to make the most of the opportunity I have in these years to teach my children to love you, follow you and seek you first in everything. In Jesus' name. Amen.

Thoughts…

Day 23

"No discipline seems pleasant at the time, but painful. Later on, however, it produces a harvest of righteousness and peace for those who have been trained by it."

- Hebrews 12:11

Discipline is certainly one of the most difficult and controversial aspects of parenting. So difficult, in fact, that it can be tempting to avoid discipline altogether and just allow your children to do whatever they want without any consequences for their behavior. I know the feeling, believe me. Training children is exhausting! From the two-year-old who continually takes her baby sister's favorite toy just to hear her scream, to the eighteen-year-old who misses curfew on a regular basis, these kids seem bound and determined to wear us down! And can I tell you a secret? They are. They have plenty of energy and nothing but time and if they can break you, they know they will be in control. There's a lot at stake here, mama, so don't you give up!

This is not just about being in control so that you can "win." Remember, you and your children are all on the same team. You are on their side. You want your children to learn respect, self-control, discipline and integrity, and if you don't teach them, who will? Not only that, if you neglect to discipline your children and train them well, they will pay for it for the rest of their lives. Don't believe me?

Consider this... When you see a teenager or young adult who doesn't show respect for authority, can't show up on time, and has no work ethic, what are your thoughts about that person? Would you want your children to be friends with him? Would you hire him? Would you even want to spend time with him? A child who is not taught discipline will be fighting an uphill battle for the rest of his life. So press on dear mama! You are doing important work.

The key to discipline is consistency. The child must understand what the consequence will be for disobedience, and that consequence must happen every time the child is defiant. Pick your battles here. Don't punish them for childish behavior or accidents, but only when your child has disobeyed a rule or direct request. Be calm, firm and loving, and help them understand that you are unhappy with their behavior but your love for them is unwavering. In fact, discipline is one way you show them love. They won't really understand it when they are young, but someday they will thank you.

We have all had those days when it seemed like all we did all day was discipline children who were being disobedient. No fun for anyone, to be sure. But please keep the big picture in mind. We are training future adults, and they need to learn these character traits from the time they are small. If your three-year-old knows she is in charge and that you don't really mean what you say, then when she is thirteen you will have a nightmare on your hands. Begin today to plant seeds for the future you want for your children.

Think and Grow:
- Do you and your husband agree on how to discipline your children?
- Are you consistent in training your children?
- What adjustments can you make now with the future in mind?

Prayer:
Oh Father, thank you for training and disciplining me when I go astray and reminding me that training is part of being a loving parent. Help me to have the diligence to train my children to honor you with their character and behavior. In Jesus' name. Amen.

Thoughts…

Day 24

"I praise you for remembering me in everything and for holding to the traditions just as I passed them on to you."

- 1 Corinthians 11:2

In our family, tradition is a powerful force. We have traditions for holidays, birthdays, seasons and other special occasions. Some traditions have been established intentionally and some have come about as a happy accident. There are some that have been with us for more than twenty years and others that have started as recently as two or three years ago. But all of our traditions draw us closer together as a family and make life fun and predictable.

Think back to your family of origin and the fond memories that remain will probably involve traditions. Those fun and special things that you did together over and over again make up the fabric of your childhood years. And now, you have the privilege of starting your own traditions for your young family.

If you think about it, I'll bet you have already begun establishing your own traditions. For us, birthdays are special. The day begins when my mom brings donuts for breakfast and the birthday person opens gifts and cards. There is always a specially requested dinner and homemade birthday cake in the evening, but nobody wants to wait that long for presents!

Homemade cinnamon rolls are a treat reserved for the mornings of Thanksgiving and Easter. We always bake lots of Christmas cookies, get up early to go Black Friday shopping and stand in line for Rita's Italian Ice on the first day of spring (even if it happens to be 40 degrees.) On our annual family vacation, the kids (ages 13-24) still love getting a goodie bag every hour on the hour during the long road trip. That was a trick I tried one year to keep them happy and cooperative during our ten-hour drive, but it stuck!

One year the kids asked if they could eat Christmas cookies for breakfast while opening their gifts, even though I had planned a fancy brunch. I couldn't really think of a good reason to say no, and now we always have cookies and hot cocoa on Christmas morning.

Listening to my family talk about our traditions and look forward to the next one is such a joyful part of this parenting journey. In many ways, traditions are the glue that hold a family together. They add to the feeling of unity and togetherness. So go ahead, start some new traditions this year. Some of them will stick, and others won't, and some won't even be your idea! But none of that matters. It's all weaving together a beautiful tapestry that becomes your unique family culture.

Think and Grow:
- What happy memories do you have of childhood traditions?
- Can you already see traditions forming in your young family?
- How can you be intentional about beginning some new traditions?

Prayer:
Dear Lord, thank you for the opportunity to build a strong family culture through shared traditions. I'm thankful for the ones I grew up with, but even more excited to begin new ones with my own family. Give me creativity and inspiration as I seek to make lasting memories for my children. And remind me to listen to their hearts too. They may just have a great idea that will become a favorite new family tradition. In Jesus' name. Amen.

Thoughts…

Day 25

"Do not let any unwholesome talk come out of
your mouths, but only what is helpful for building
others up according to their needs, that it may
benefit those who listen."

- Ephesians 4:29

Do we use our words to build up our
children or to tear them down? Probably some
of each, if we're honest. In our calmest and best
moments we are kind, loving and patient with our
children and it's easy to speak words of love and
life to them. But in our most frazzled, stressed
out, sleep deprived moments it is far too easy to
spew venomous words we immediately wish we
could take back. If this hits home for you, please
don't beat yourself up about it, but let's learn and
grow and pray together so that we can do better
next time.

So many Bible verses refer to the tongue
and its power to accomplish good or evil. God
must have known (of course he did) that we
would all struggle with the words that escape
from our lips sometimes. Several of these
verses, including Ephesians 4:29, were made
into posters on our kitchen wall many times as
our children were growing up. They served as
ever-present reminders of the importance of self

control when we speak. The children needed to be reminded daily, but so did their mom!

Mamas, we need to grasp the weight that our words carry with our children. Can you remember hurtful words spoken to you when you were a child? Of course, we all can. But when those words come from a parent, they have even more power to wound a tender heart.

If you are struggling with your temper, make it a priority to get it under control. Search for Bible verses to hang around your house as reminders, find books and Bible studies to read, talk to a trusted friend or mentor for advice and accountability and above all, pray for God's help in controlling your tongue. Your words are so important, especially with your children.

When we slip up in the heat of the moment and say something hurtful, the best way to deal with it is to go back to your child after you have calmed down and apologize. Explain that you didn't mean what you said, you were angry and you were wrong. Then ask for forgiveness. Believe me, I know that this can be difficult and very humbling, but it will restore the relationship in a way that nothing else can. You will also be setting a wonderful example for your children to follow when they say or do something they regret.

Look, as much as we would like to be perfectly holy, we are all still works in progress. The goal is to have fewer and fewer incidents to apologize for as the Holy Spirit does his work in us. But in the meantime, we can learn to apologize when we blow it, and teach our children to do the same.

Think and Grow:
- Did any unwholesome talk come out of your mouth today? This week?
- Have you used words to intentionally build up your children and meet their needs?
- Do you need to apologize to your child and ask forgiveness for misspoken words?

Prayer:
Father God, forgive me for all the unwholesome talk that has come out of my mouth, especially when it has been directed at my children. You have given me these precious gifts to care for and my desire is to build them up according to their needs. Lord, you know I need your help with that every day. Please give me the courage and humility I need to apologize when I fail. May the words spoken in our home honor each other and you. In Jesus' name. Amen.

Thoughts…

Maximize Your Marriage

Day 26

"The Lord God said, 'It is not good for the man to be alone. I will make a helper suitable for him.'"
- Genesis 2:18

Way back at the very beginning of the Bible, as God was creating the heavens and the earth, the moon and the stars, the animals and plants, he concluded that busy week by creating a man. Up until this point, he had declared everything that he created to be "good." But suddenly there was something that was "not good." The man should not be alone. That's not good. So God created a woman to be a suitable helper for him. And that was good.

In the same way, God has created you, in part, to be a helper suitable for your husband if you are married. For some of us (myself included) this is an adjustment. In today's world, a woman can be just about anything she wants to be, and being a wife may be just one of her many titles. Sometimes we can lose sight of the fact that being a wife is not just a role, but also a calling. In fact, if you are married, then God has called you to be the best wife you can be to your husband. This includes helping him, meeting his needs and spending time with him.

The season of raising small children may be the most challenging time in a marriage. The demands on your time are never ending, you are probably sleep deprived and exhausted, and by the time the children are asleep you may not have an ounce of energy left to think about being a helper to your husband. But remember, you were his wife before you were a mother. And after your children are grown and have their own lives, your husband (Lord willing) will still be by your side for years to come.

It is absolutely imperative that you keep building your relationship with him throughout these years of child rearing. Of course, it may look different from when you were courting or newly married. You will need to get creative and make the most of the time, money and energy you have available in this season, but it will be worth it.

Make time for a "date night" at least once or twice a month. Arrange for child care and get away together to reconnect and really check in with each other.

Life at home may be hectic, but you can still keep your bond strong on a daily basis. Always kiss him goodbye in the morning and greet him warmly when he comes home. Ask him how his day was and really listen to the answer.

Make his favorite foods regularly and ask him what you can do for him each day. Even if he can't think of anything, he will appreciate the fact that you offered.

The way we care for our home and children is another way we can be a helper suitable for him. Even in the 21st century, your husband would love to come home to a peaceful, well maintained house and enjoy a nice dinner with his family. You can provide those blessings for him and strengthen your marriage at the same time.

Think and Grow:
- Do you think of yourself as a helper to your husband?
- When was the last time the two of you had some time alone together?
- What steps can you take to make your calling as his wife a top priority in your life?

Prayer:
Father, thank you for the reminder today that you have created me to be my husband's best helper. Show me ways that I can improve in that role. Give me the wisdom and energy to make my husband's needs a priority from this day forward. In Jesus' name. Amen.

Thoughts…

Day 27

"Love is patient, love is kind. It does not envy, it does not boast, it is not proud. It does not dishonor others, it is not self-seeking, it is not easily angered, it keeps no record of wrongs. Love does not delight in evil but rejoices with the truth. It always protects, always trusts, always hopes, always perseveres. Love never fails."
- 1 Corinthians 13:4-8

Chances are good that these verses were part of your wedding ceremony. On that day you believed in the power of these words and were excited to put them into practice. But then...life happened. It's hard to be patient when your husband tracks mud through the house again, or continues to throw his dirty socks on the floor beside the hamper (not that I would know).

Being kind is difficult when you are trying to clean the kitchen and wrangle the kiddos into the bathtub while he sits and watches the game. And maybe the most difficult part of all is keeping no record of wrongs. When a disagreement surfaces, it is so tempting to remind him of all the things he has done to hurt you in the past.

It's not easy to love the way God tells us we should love. We're not talking about the honeymoon kind of love, this is love in the trenches of everyday life. It's about putting someone else's needs ahead of your own. And above all, it perseveres.

I'm sure you've heard it said that the best thing you can do for your children is to love their dad. It seems obvious that we would love our husbands, and most of us would not hesitate to say that we do, but what do our actions communicate? Love is not a feeling, but a choice we make each and every day to act in a loving way. Read over today's passage again. Do these words describe how you relate to your husband on a daily basis? Maybe it would be a good idea to write it down and put it on your bathroom mirror as a daily reminder. Just think how our marriages would be transformed if we took these words to heart in each interaction with our spouse.

If you realize that you haven't been loving your husband well according to this scripture, you know what you need to do, right? It's time for an apology. Go to your husband in humility and confess that you have not been as loving to him as you would like to be and ask his forgiveness.

If your marriage has been strained lately, this could be the beginning of a beautiful transformation for both of you. Tell him that you want to build a great marriage and that you are willing to keep on trying because love always hopes and always perseveres. Then decide together what steps you can take to show God's kind of love to each other.

Think and Grow:
- Which of the words in these verses do you have the most trouble living out?
- Which word are you most consistent in showing? Celebrate that!
- What steps can you take to be more loving toward your husband?

Prayer:
Father, I know I love my husband, but after studying your description of love, I'm not so sure I'm good at communicating that love to him. Forgive me for all the times I've fallen short. Help me not to feel guilty or condemned, but to be proactive about improving my marriage. Show me where to start, I need your help. In Jesus' name. Amen.

Thoughts…

Day 28

"However, each one of you also must love his wife as he loves himself, and the wife must respect her husband."

- Ephesians 5:33

The wife must respect her husband. "Well, what if he acts like a jerk?" The wife must respect her husband. "What if he loses his job and can't provide for us?" The wife must respect her husband. "What if today I can't think of one thing about him that is respectable?" The wife must respect her husband. "Wait a minute, isn't respect something that needs to be earned?" The wife must respect her husband. The day you said, "I do," you agreed to respect your husband for as long as you both shall live. For some of us, respecting our husbands may be even harder than loving them, but God's word gives us no choice. A man needs respect and he needs it most of all from his wife.

So what does it look like to respect your husband in the midst of everyday life? I'm sure you can think of lots of ways, and every husband is unique, but there are a few things all of us can do:

- Praise him sincerely, especially in front of other people. Notice what he does for his family and call it to everyone's attention.
- Encourage your children to respect their dad. Remember, you get to set the example. "Didn't Daddy do a great job washing the car? Look how shiny it is!"
- Ask for his opinion and heed his advice. Show him respect by listening to his preferences and remembering what he likes and what he doesn't.
- Remember to thank him for all that he does for you and your family.
- "I'm proud of you" is the most powerful phrase you can say to him.

On the other hand, disrespecting a husband is one of the most destructive things we can do, yet it can happen before we have time to think. How often do we roll our eyes, make a snide comment or dismiss his opinion without a second thought? I shudder to think how many times those things have happened in our house. Remember, our kids are watiching. If we act like their daddy is the greatest man in the world, chances are good that they will too.

If you struggle with this issue, I want to challenge you to try an experiment. Commit to treating your husband with nothing but respect for a week. I understand that if you are not feeling loved by him it will be a difficult task, but we are on a mission to glorify God. At the end of the week, see if the atmosphere in your marriage has changed. And by all means, don't give up after just a week!

Giving a man the respect he so desperately needs can be like giving oxygen to someone who is suffocating. You may just discover that you have a whole new husband...or that you have the old one back again.

Think and Grow:
- Can you think of a time recently when you showed respect to your husband?
- Was there a time when you disrespected him?
- Take the one-week respect challenge and see what happens.

Prayer:

Father, sometimes I read a verse in the Bible and I wish it weren't quite so clear. The wife must respect her husband. Ouch. Please forgive me for the times when I've fallen short of your best for my marriage. Help me to treat my husband with respect every day, not only to honor him, but also to honor you. In Jesus' name. Amen.

Thoughts…

Day 29

"Better to live in a desert than with a quarrelsome and nagging wife."
                                    - Proverbs 21:19

What would it be like to live in a desert? (Remember, the Bible was written before modern conveniences like air conditioning.) Some words that come to mind are hot, dry, desolate, scorching, lonely, barren and dangerous. Imagine living in a vast wasteland with no water or shelter from the scorching heat. Sounds awful, right? Who in their right mind would choose to live in those conditions? No one except a husband who had to choose between that desert and a quarrelsome and nagging wife.

Leave it to the Word of God to just tell it like it is. Ladies, we're keepin' it real today. Nagging and quarreling are two different things, but they have the same affect on your husband. Both leave him feeling like the two of you are not on the same team.

Of course, there are times when you and your husband will disagree, and that's okay! I'm not telling you not to express your opinion and your viewpoint. As your husband's helper, that is part of your job description. Two heads are better than one, and many times you will be able to help him see the big picture more clearly by sharing your thoughts.

But there is a way to discuss difficult issues without being argumentative. If a discussion suddenly starts to feel more like a quarrel, take a timeout and cool off. Pray for wisdom and remember that you are both on the same team. The goal isn't to "win" the disagreement, but to come to a decision together without damaging the relationship.

What does nagging sound like? Drip, drip, drip... Have you ever had to "remind" your husband about something you had already talked about? Something that needed to be fixed, an errand you asked him to run or a behavior you hoped he could change? (Hello, dirty socks, there on the floor next to the hamper.) Maybe you have learned, like I have, that repeating yourself with an increasingly irritated tone of voice does not get you any closer to your goal. In fact, it probably causes feelings of irritation and resentment instead.

A far better option is to pray and ask God for his wisdom. Maybe he will show you that the issue isn't worth the trouble it's causing and help you let go. Or perhaps he will provide an opportunity for you both to discuss the issue in a calm and loving manner. Either way, avoiding nagging is worth the effort.

Every couple has disagreements...that's just part of life and marriage. The key to a healthy marriage is to deal with these conflicts in a loving and respectful way. That way, no matter the outcome, everybody wins.

Think and Grow:
- Would you consider yourself to be quarrelsome? Would your husband?
- Can you think of a time when you have nagged your hubby?
- What steps can you take to deal differently with issues in the future?

Prayer:
Father, thank you for blessing me with my husband. Help me to remember, on those days when we are not seeing eye to eye, that he is a gift from you. Teach me to approach conflicts carefully and with the respect he needs. I don't ever want to be a quarrelsome or nagging wife to him, so help me to see what needs to change in my attitudes, words and actions. Thank you for always leading me along the right path. In Jesus' name. Amen.

Thoughts…

Day 30

"A wife of noble character, who can find? She is worth far more than rubies. Her husband has full confidence in her and lacks nothing of value. She brings him good, not harm, all the days of her life... Charm is deceptive, and beauty is fleeting; but a woman who fears the Lord is to be praised."

- Proverbs 31:10-12, 30

It seems only fitting that we should end our 30 days together with more wisdom from Proverbs 31, the ultimate passage about what it looks like to be a godly wife and mother. It all comes down to cultivating a noble character, a mission that will take a lifetime to accomplish. Every step of the way we are learning and growing into the women God created us to be. And as we grow, we are becoming like a rare and precious jewel, worth far more than rubies!

Think how happy your husband will be to have full confidence in you. And why? Because you bring him good and not harm all the days of your life. So that even when the beauty of your youth has faded, he will still praise you as a treasured woman who fears the Lord.

In order to become all you can be as a woman, wife and mother, you will always be learning. Reading the Bible and other good books, spending time with other godly women you admire, and seeking God's will for your life through prayer will become daily habits that will transform you little by little. As you choose to invest your time and money wisely, you will see rewards. As you nurture your health and faith you will have hope for a bright future. And as you give your best to your marriage and motherhood, your family will rise up and call you blessed.

This season of mothering little ones feels like it will never end, but you know it will. Every day they grow and become just a bit more independent. Before you know it, you'll be taking them to college or walking them down the aisle and wondering where the time went. So, dear mommy, I challenge you to make the choice each day to maximize motherhood.

Choose to put distractions aside and soak in every moment; to speak words of life and faith to their hearts while they're still listening. Choose to nurture yourself and your marriage so that you can give them the best mom and dad possible. And choose to make wise decisions with your resources for today and for the future, because it's coming faster than you think.

Remember, your little ones are watching you and learning from you every moment, so take great care to live wisely. They learn more from what you do than from what you say, and they spell love T-I-M-E. Be there for them as much as possible when they are young. It won't be long before they will want to be with friends more than family, so capitalize on the opportunity you have today. Believe me when I tell you, there will be plenty of time to pursue other interests and goals when they are older. Right now, motherhood is your most pressing priority.

You are doing a great work.

And you are doing a great job!

Prayer:

Thank you, Lord, for the gift of motherhood. This life is beautiful and crazy, frustrating and magical, exciting and exhausting, all at the same time. The desire of my heart is to be the best mother possible to my children, but I know that will only happen as I learn to rely on you for strength and wisdom each and every moment of this journey. Help me to focus on what is most important in this season, and let go of things that can wait. I have such a short window of influence with my children, Lord. Help me to maximize motherhood while I can. In Jesus' name. Amen.

Thoughts…

Thank you for spending these 30 days with me exploring what it means to maximize motherhood. Or, if your life is like mine was when my children were little, maybe it took you a bit longer than 30 days. No judgment here. Give yourself grace. My hope and prayer is that you'll pull this devotional book out and go through it time and time again and that God will use it to instruct, encourage and bless you for years to come.

I would love to hear your thoughts, questions, and what you're learning along the way.

I'm also available to speak at women's events, MOPS groups and retreats.

*For more information about the life-changing health supplements I've discovered, email your questions, contact info and any health issues you struggle with and I'll be happy to help you.

You can contact me at
maximizemotherhood@gmail.com

Love, prayers and many blessings,
Deb

Made in the USA
Middletown, DE
20 December 2016